Earth's Changing Climate

Food, Water, and Climate Change

World Book
a Scott Fetzer company
Chicago

For information about other World Book publications, visit our website at www.worldbook.com or call 1-800-WORLDBK (967-5325).

For information about sales to schools and libraries, call 1-800-975-3250 (United States) or 1-800-837-5365 (Canada).

World Book, Inc.
180 North LaSalle Street
Suite 900
Chicago, Illinois 60601
USA

Library of Congress Cataloging-in-Publication Data
Title: Food, water, and climate change.
Description: Chicago: World Book, a Scott Fetzer Company, [2016] | Series:
    Earth's changing climate | Includes index.
Identifiers: LCCN 2015029792 | ISBN 9780716627128
Subjects: LCSH: Food security--Juvenile literature. | Food supply--Juvenile
    literature. | Water supply--Juvenile literature. | Climatic changes--Juvenile literature.
Classification: LCC HD9000.5 .F668 2016 | DDC 363.8--dc23
LC record available at http://lccn.loc.gov/2015029792

Earth's Changing Climate
ISBN: 978-0-7166-2705-0 (set, hc.)

Also available as:
ISBN: 978-0-7166-2722-7 (e-book, ePUB3)

Printed in China by Toppan Leefung Printing Ltd., Guangdong Province
2nd printing August 2016

Staff

Writer: Edward Ricciuti

Executive Committee

President
Jim O'Rourke

Vice President and
Editor in Chief
Paul A. Kobasa

Vice President, Finance
Donald D. Keller

Vice President, Marketing
Jean Lin

Director, Human Resources
Bev Ecker

Editorial

Director of Digital Product
Content Development
Emily Kline

Manager, Science
Jeff De La Rosa

Editors, Science
Will Adams
Echo Gonzalez

Administrative Assistant
Annuals/Series Nonfiction
Ethel Matthews

Manager, Contracts &
Compliance (Rights &
Permissions)
Loranne K. Shields

Manager, Indexing Services
David Pofelski

Digital

Director of Digital Product
Development
Erika Meller

Digital Product Manager
Lyndsie Manusos

Digital Product Coordinator
Matthew Werner

**Manufacturing/
Production**

Manufacturing Manager
Sandra Johnson

Production/Technology
Manager
Anne Fritzinger

Proofreader
Nathalie Strassheim

Graphics and Design

Senior Art Director
Tom Evans

Senior Designers
Matt Carrington
Isaiah Sheppard
Don Di Sante

Senior Cartographer
John M. Rejba

Acknowledgments

Alamy Images: 7 (Sean Pavone), 17 (Jose More, VWPics), 19 (Nigel Cattlin), 31 (WaterFrame), 35 (Christian Goupi, age fotostock). Getty Images: 33 (Danita Delimont), 37 (Jeff Rotman), 43 (Carla Gottgens, Bloomberg). Shutterstock: 5 (Chatrawee Wiratgasem), 9 (Tuanjai Pratumma), 11 (jeka84), 13 (welcomia), 15 (CHAINFOTO24), 21 (Ivankibo), 23 (Martinho Smart), 25 (Berzina), 27 (Andrew Astbury), 29 (Jaromir Chalabala), 39 (Shawn Hempel), 41 (Peter Kunasz), 45 (Baloncici).

Table of contents

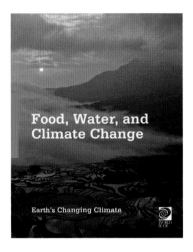

Sunrise over farm fields in Yuanyang, China.

© Aloxey/Shutterstock

Glossary There is a glossary of terms on page 46. Terms defined in the glossary are in type **that looks like this** on their first appearance on any spread (two facing pages).

Introduction

An extreme cold snap strikes the windy grasslands high in the Andes Mountains of Peru. Farmers there who raise camel-like alpacas (al PAK uhz) for wool lose their herds to the bitter cold. The worst **drought** (drowt) in years dries out the humid lowlands of Thailand in Southeast Asia. Without rain, rice farmers cannot flood their fields and plant their crop. Off the western coast of South Africa, a sardine fisherman's net comes up empty. The fish have moved away to escape warming ocean temperatures. In a wealthy California *suburb* (a town near a major city), a homeowner complains because her community has banned the watering of lawns. **Reservoirs** (REHZ uhr vwahrz) that supply water to her town are low because too little snow fell in the high mountains to fill them during the spring melt.

As Earth warms, people everywhere find that climate change threatens their ability to get food and water. Eighty percent of the world's farmable land is already in use. Experts predict that crop production in coming years could drop by 25 percent due to climate change. The world's poor will be hit hardest by the warming.

This book explores the challenges to providing food and water in a warming world and how people are *adapting* (changing) to meet them.

Farmers planting rice in a
flooded field in Asia

Population growth

In nature, animal populations go up and down over time. If a population grows too large for available food and water, many of its animals will die. **Predators** and disease also reduce numbers. For most of history, the human population was affected by the same rules as animals. Advances in medicine have changed things for humans. Today, humans, on average, live decades longer than they did thousands of years ago.

There are more than 7 billion people on Earth today—about 1 billion more than in the year 2000 and seven times more than in 1950. By the end of this century, according to a United Nations estimate, Earth's human population could reach 10 billion people. Such a population will stretch supplies of food and water to the limit. Many regions already do not have enough clean, fresh water. And, while the world grows enough food to feed everyone, food supplies are not divided up equally. Most of the world's hungry have no land on which to grow food. Much of the land they do have is useless for farming.

Today, even with modern **technology,** providing enough food and water for all of us is difficult. It will be even more difficult as the **climate** changes and weather patterns shift.

Many people live in a very small area in Osaka, Japan.

The effect of population on climate change

Energy has been called the "master resource." It takes energy to produce and deliver such other resources as food and water. The United States Energy Information Administration (EIA) reports that by 2040, the increased human population will require at least 50 percent more energy to supply its needs than we use today. Eighty percent of that energy will come from **fossil fuels**: oil, coal, and natural gas.

Burning fossil fuels adds huge amounts of **carbon dioxide** (CO_2) gas to the **atmosphere.** Carbon dioxide helps trap heat near Earth's surface, warming the planet like a greenhouse. Adding more CO_2 to the atmosphere increases this greenhouse effect, raising **average temperatures** worldwide. Without restrictions, the EIA reports that the amount of CO_2 added to the atmosphere will increase 46 percent from 2010 to 2040.

Plants and trees absorb CO_2 from the air to make food and build their tall trunks and leaves. Logging and clearing land for farms is destroying forests in many regions, especially the **tropics.** Almost half the forests in the west African country of Nigeria were cleared between 1995 and 2005. Indonesia, an island nation in Southeast Asia, has lost more than 20 percent of its forestland, and there are plans to clear much more. By clearing land, people help bring about more warming.

Global warming vs. climate change

The words *global warming* and *climate change* are often used to mean the same thing. These words are used to mean two very closely linked ideas. Global warming is the recent, *observed* (noticed) increase in **average global surface temperatures** on Earth. Climate change means the changes in **climate** linked to changes in average global temperature. Global average temperature has a complicated effect on climate. Global warming will not cause every place to get warmer. Instead, it will have a variety of effects on temperature, rain and snow, and other parts of climate. These effects are together called *climate change*.

A photo from Thailand, a country in Southeast Asia, shows land on a mountain where a forest was cleared so that crops could be planted.

The food supply

Four crops supply 75 percent of the world's food: corn (or maize), wheat, rice, and soybeans. Harvests of all these crops are threatened by global warming. Even a small rise in temperatures can damage crops. When corn and rice plants produce flowers, they are particularly at risk from a jump in temperature. For wheat, too much warmth *stunts* (slows or stops) its growth. Warming also encourages the growth of insect pests, disease, and weeds that can further reduce crop production.

Related to global warming, rising **sea levels** and increasingly powerful storms threaten crops, especially in the **tropics.** Floods from **cyclones** bring ocean water inland, making drinking water too salty for 20 million people in Bangladesh, a country in South Asia. By the year 2090, southern Bangladesh could lose 40 percent of its cropland to a rise in sea level. Meanwhile, other areas could end up without enough water due to shifting rain patterns.

Warming may benefit such northern nations as Canada. A longer frost-free growing season due to warming could allow for increased crop production. But, summers that are too hot could threaten livestock and poultry. Extreme floods and **droughts** could eventually cut Canadian harvests by half.

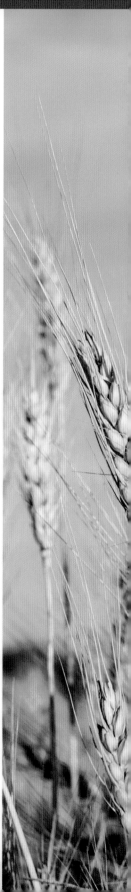

Drought threatens wheat crops in many regions.

California's fruit trees

California, on the Pacific coast of the United States, leads all states in the production of food. Its farmers raise more than 400 different crops. Almost half the vegetables, fruits, and nuts grown in the United States are California grown. California is the only U.S. producer of more than a dozen crops, including almonds, dates, and walnuts. It is a major producer of many other crops, including avocados, lemons, peaches, plums, and grapes.

During the dry summer, crops in California need **irrigation.** The water used comes from snow that falls in winter on the nearby Sierra Nevada and Cascade mountains. In spring, the snowpack—the build-up of snow over the winter—slowly melts and is collected in **reservoirs.** Recently, California has seen its driest and hottest years ever recorded. Warmer winters mean rain falls instead of snow. Unlike snow, rain drains off the land quickly and is lost. Higher temperatures also shrink the mountain snowpack, which melts too early and too fast. As a result, reservoirs are at record lows. If the **drought** continues, farmers will need more irrigation. However, water will be even scarcer.

A lemon orchard in California

13

Thailand's rice fields

No country provides more rice to the world than Thailand. The Thai government sometimes even limits the harvest to control the price of rice on world markets. However, as 2015 began, so did Thailand's worst **drought** in a decade. The drought signals that, in the future, another force beyond governmental control may affect Thailand's rice crop: climate change due to global warming.

Thailand's rice crop is grown in fields flooded during the rainy season, which occurs from late spring to early fall. Later in the year, farmers **irrigate** their fields for a second crop. But climate change brings unpredictable weather that upsets this schedule. Early drought kills young rice plants, while heavy rains at season's end ruin the harvest. Rising **sea levels** resulting from global warming can flood farmland along the coast. Scientists also worry that a rise in sea level could put the country's capitol, Bangkok, under water.

Thailand is exploring ways to protect the city and the rice crop. These include flood barriers, growing rice on higher ground, and breeding varieties of rice that can grow in warmer weather.

This rice field in Thailand is ready for harvest.

Urban farming

Moving food from farms to towns and cities is expensive. In addition, **carbon dioxide** (CO_2) produced by trucks adds to warming. So, community groups and businesses in some areas are changing rooftops, empty lots, and floating *barges* (boats) into *urban* (city) farms. Crops on these farms are grown in containers filled with soil. In many cities, these farms create a new use for old, empty buildings.

Inside such buildings, plants are stacked up on racks, often floor by floor. **LED lights** may substitute for sunlight on these "vertical farms." Plants often are grown indoors using *hydroponics* (HY druh PON ihkz). In hydroponics, the plants are grown in liquid instead of soil.

Urban farming is seen all over the world. Philadelphia, a city in the eastern United States, has more than 400 community gardens. The Chinese region of Hong Kong has about 300. A farm within a huge building in Japan produces millions of lettuce plants a year under 17,500 LED lights.

In 2015, British scientists discovered that helpful insects, such as bees, do as well in cities as they do in the country. In fact, more types of wild plants were found growing in the cities studied compared to the countryside.

An urban farm with beehives (the stacked boxes) on the rooftop of Chicago's City Hall

Fish and farms

Aquarium (fish tank) owners frequently change the water in their fish tank to a prevent buildup of waste, mostly from fish and uneaten food. The waste is loaded with *nutrients* (substances that help living things grow). Poured on houseplants, tank water provides fertilizer and moisture. Some urban farmers have caught on to this idea. They raise fish for market and use the waste water on their crops.

Can scientists help plants adapt to a new climate?

Scientists have changed the **genes** of many plants so they are easier to grow and have more value. One *variety* (special kind) of corn has received genes from a **bacteria** that helps it to resist a serious pest, the European corn borer. In another example, a variety of rice with genes from corn produces vitamin A, an important nutrient that standard rice lacks. Many people who depend on rice as their main food do not get enough vitamin A.

Scientists are adding genes to rice to combat the effects of **climate** change. Flooding kills rice plants if they are under water for four or more days. Scientists have discovered a gene that lets a new type of rice survive floods for more than two weeks. Another new rice variety is not harmed by salt from ocean flooding. Added genes help another variety to survive **drought.** Scientists are also trying to find genes that prevent rice, wheat, peas, and soybeans from losing nutrients when **carbon dioxide** levels in the **atmosphere** rise.

Some people are against adding new genes to food plants. They worry about the effects to our health and the environment. Many scientists, however, feel that plants changed in this way are little different than traditional crop plants, which have been changed through thousands of years of selective breeding.

A scientist studies a rice crop being used in experiments.

Producing meat in a changing climate

People everywhere get food from animals, both wild and farm-raised. Meat, milk, and eggs are key sources of **protein** and other nutrients for millions of people worldwide.

Changing climate creates problems for people who raise livestock. Animals are healthiest when their body temperature stays the same. When temperatures rise and fall quickly, it may cause changes to an animal's behavior and the way its body works. Pigs lose weight. Chickens may stop laying eggs. Cows or goats may produce less milk.

Climate change also can spread diseases and pests. Heavy rain right after a dry spell triggers the growth of the **bacteria** that cause *anthrax*, a disease that can be deadly to livestock and people. Wet summers trigger the spread of lungworm, which strikes farm animals and such wildlife as deer.

Increased warmth and moisture that happens with climate change may allow weeds to spread into new regions. They can then grow in new pastures and crops grown to feed animals.

Livestock and climate change

Cows burp a lot. They also pass gas regularly. The gas they expel in both cases is **methane.** A cow *emits* (gives off) up to 50 gallons (200 liters) of methane daily, mostly from burps. Methane is produced by *microorganisms* (tiny living things, such as **bacteria**) that aid digestion in a cow's stomach. There are around 1.5 billion cows in the world, and they pump a lot of methane into the **atmosphere.** Methane is a "greenhouse gas" that, like **carbon dioxide,** traps heat in the atmosphere.

According to the United Nations Food and Agricultural Organization, cows and other livestock give off more greenhouse gas than all of the *vehicles* (cars and trucks, for example) driven. Methane does not remain in the atmosphere as long as carbon dioxide does. But, it absorbs heat faster.

Scientists hope to reduce methane produced by cows through changes in their diet. Some promise has been shown by adding garlic, cinnamon, cashew shells, and oregano to cattle feed. Methane from cow manure is already being collected for use as fuel.

Cattle graze in a meadow.

Alpaca farms

South America's Altiplano (Spanish for "high plain")
is the world's second-highest **plateau.** At almost
15,000 feet (4,500 meters) high, it lies mostly in the
countries of Peru and Bolivia, between the eastern
and western Andes mountains. Few trees grow on
this dry, flat land. Some parts of the Altiplano get
only 6 inches (15 centimeters) of rain a year. It is
cold. Even on a summer day, the temperature can
drop well below freezing at night. **Oxygen** levels
are so low that people new to the high *altitudes*
(heights) find it difficult to breathe.

It is difficult to make a living on the Altiplano.
Nothing much except tough grasses, *quinoa* (KEE
noh ah—a type of grain), and potatoes grow there.
People depend on camel-like *alpacas* for meat,
milk, and wool. Recently, unusual weather caused
by climate change has put these hardy animals at
risk, especially their young. Freezing temperatures
have come three months early. Summers have
become hotter and drier, killing the grasses that the
alpaca eat. In other months, extra moisture in the
atmosphere has brought flooding and early snows.

The wild weather has caused the deaths of
thousands of alpacas and destroyed potato and
quinoa crops. Climate change is making a hard life
harder than ever for people of the Altiplano.

An alpaca on the
Altiplano in Bolivia

Arctic hunters

The Inuit (IHN yu iht) people of the Arctic (an area that centers on the North Pole) hunt land and sea animals for food, clothing, shelter, and tools. Higher temperatures, melting **sea ice,** and changing patterns of rain and snow threaten Arctic animals and the entire **ecosystem,** as well as the Inuit way of life.

Ringed seals and bearded seals bear and raise young in snow dens on the ice. Melting earlier in the season caused by warming temperatures collapses dens, sometimes killing the pups.

On land, red foxes are moving north and killing Arctic foxes. The red foxes can now move north because climate change has made the **habitat** of the Arctic fox warm enough for them to live in, as well.

The plantlike lichens (LY kuhnz) eaten by *caribou* (KAR uh boo—a type of large deer) are killed by the summer **drought** and fires encouraged by high temperatures. The warmer temperatures also increase moisture in the air during winter, increasing snowfall. Caribou then have to struggle to dig for lichens through heavy snow.

Arctic foxes are threatened by red foxes moving north into their habitat.

27

The high cost of meat

As Earth's population grows, farmers must grow as much food as possible from the land. One way to do this is to grow more plant foods and raise fewer animals for meat. Plants can feed more people than can crops grown to feed livestock on the same amount of land. Livestock and crops to feed them take up more than a third of Earth's land. Food crops for people cover only a little more than one-tenth of Earth's land. With climate change, some of the land used for crops and livestock is being threatened.

Most of the food that Americans get from corn is not the corn itself. Instead, it is from dairy and meat from animals who are fed the corn. It takes 40 percent of the corn crop to feed the animals that supply those items. Beyond that, another 40 percent of the corn crop goes to make fuel. Only about 10 percent of the United States corn crop is used directly for food. Much of that is used for corn syrup sweeteners. The corn could feed five times the number of people it does if it went straight to the dinner table.

Americans and Europeans get most of their **protein** from meat. In other parts of the world, such as Africa and Asia, for example, many people get most of their protein from plants and fish. To feed everyone in the coming years, people in developed countries may have to eat less meat so more food is available.

A woman in Sri Lanka serves a traditional meal without meat.

Meat eaters

People in South Asian nations eat far less meat than do Americans. In India, for example, people eat, on average, about 2 pounds (5 kilograms) of meat yearly. An average American, on the other hand, eats 58 pounds (127 kilograms) each year.

Harvesting fish in a changing climate

People eat more than 110 million tons (100 million metric tons) of fish a year. Fish provide 2.5 billion people with 20 percent of the **protein** in their diet. Four billion more get 15 percent of their protein from fish. People in some poorer countries get half of their daily protein from fish.

Earth's supply of fish is shrinking, in part because of climate change. Ocean waters are warming. Seawater *salinity* (saltiness) is decreasing due to ice melt. High temperatures also lower the amount of **oxygen** in the water. Fish must work harder to push water over their gills, leaving less energy for growth. A study of 600 *species* (kinds) of ocean fish by Canada's University of British Columbia suggests that catches could shrink 20 percent by the year 2050 due to warming alone.

Fish farms (see photo at right) supply almost half of all the fish and shellfish we eat. Many people believe such farms may help solve problems caused by **overfishing** and global warming. But there are some problems. For example, diseases can spread quickly through fish in crowded sea cages and then spread to wild fish. The future of offshore fish farming is still unclear.

A fish farm in
the Adriatic Sea,
east of Italy

West Africa's fisheries

Such fish as snappers, groupers, sardines, mackerel, and anchovies make West African waters some of the world's most important **fisheries.** It is not surprising that fish is the most important part of the diet for many people there. People in the nation of Ghana eat 270,000 tons (300,000 metric tons) of fish a year. Fishing provides jobs and income. The catch from the countries of Cape Verde, Guinea-Bissau, Liberia, Senegal, and Sierra Leone is worth $2.5 billion. In Senegal alone, fishing supports 82,000 fishermen and 37,000 people in other jobs.

Those figures, from the World Bank, are for legal fishing. **Overfishing,** much of it done illegally from foreign boats, is harming fish populations.

Climate change also reduces fish numbers. Changes to the water temperatures change upwelling. Upwelling happens during certain seasons when winds blow aside surface waters near the coast. The colder bottom waters, which are rich in *nutrients* (nourishing things), then rise to the surface. This upwelling provides nutrients for the growth of tiny animals that fish feed on, promoting the growth of fish populations. If winds change and upwelling stops, fish populations drop sharply.

Local fishermen work on their boats in Ghana.

Traditional methods

Once a week, usually on Tuesday, fishermen in Ghana stayed ashore. According to their traditional beliefs, the sea is a sacred place. So they left the sea and its creatures at peace for a day. For centuries this custom has helped to prevent overfishing. But it may not work much longer. Large commercial (owned by business) boats have entered the field. The competition for catch is so great that most people now fish every day. The ancient methods of fish **conservation** are failing.

Louisiana's crayfish farmers

Crayfish (or crawfish) are freshwater relatives of lobsters. They are a popular food in many places. This is especially true in Louisiana, a coastal state in the south-central United States. The state produces—and eats—most of the world's crayfish. In a good year, the crayfish industry adds $300 million to Louisiana's economy. But not all years are good.

In 2005, **storm surges** from hurricanes Rita and Katrina flooded ponds in which farmers grow crayfish. Seawater killed so many crayfish that the 2006 harvest dropped by two-thirds. Even without storms, the sea is edging into Louisiana farms. The **sea level** is rising due to global warming. Meanwhile, building projects have destroyed **marshes** that shield land from the sea. This one-two punch is threatening crayfish farms along Louisiana's coast.

Farmers often grow crayfish alongside rice. They drain ponds to harvest rice in summer, when crayfish shelter from the heat in burrows. Changes in air pressure associated with summer storms trigger crayfish breeding. Farmers flood the ponds in the fall when the young crayfish emerge from their burrows. They are harvested when grown, about three months later. Climate change from warming causes too much rain or too little at the wrong time. This upsets the crayfish life cycle and shrinks the harvest.

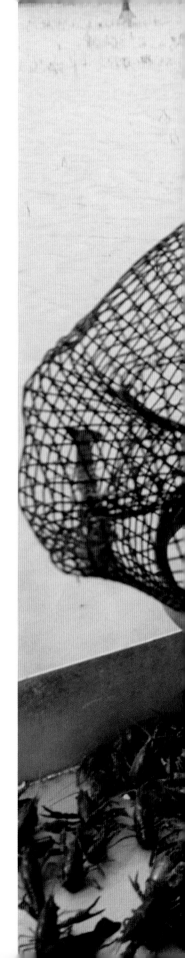

A crayfish farmer and his harvest in Louisiana

Does eating fish damage the oceans more?

Climate change caused by global warming (see page 6) is redrawing the map of where fish live. Many types of fish move towards cooler waters as the ocean warms. The oceans in the **tropics** stand to lose the most.

Even without climate change, ocean **fisheries** are declining. Oil spills and other pollution reduce fish numbers by killing fish and destroying **habitat.** The huge demand for fish as food is perhaps the greatest problem of all. **Overfishing** is the greatest threat to fisheries and even the ocean **ecosystem.** More than half the world's fisheries lack enough fish to support present catch levels. Bigger ships, huge nets, and fish-finding devices allow people to catch fish faster than the animals can *reproduce* (have more young). Huge fishing fleets from developed nations sweep one area of the ocean clean and move on to the next.

Conservationists promote *sustainable* fishing. It places limits on catches that allow fish enough time to reproduce. The establishment of no-fishing areas helps, as does international cooperation to manage catches. Individuals can help by eating only fish from sustainable fisheries.

Illegal fishing makes all this difficult. It accounts for at least one-fifth of the fish sold. Sustainable fishing will not work unless the illegal overfishing stops.

Huge commercial fishing vessels catch thousands of fish in giant nets.

The impact of global warming on fresh water

Water covers 72 percent of Earth's surface. All but 3 percent of that water is salty ocean seawater, unfit for drinking or **irrigation.** Ways to take salt out of seawater cost a lot of money. Shifting rainfall patterns due to climate change have a huge effect on the supply of fresh water.

Global warming upsets Earth's water cycle—the cycle on Earth as water moves from the oceans to the sky to the land. Some places get less rain, others get too much. For example, seasonal rains are shifting away from the western United States. Many western states may face decades of **drought.** Meanwhile, eastern U.S. states are soaked by more rain than usual.

It seems strange, but too much rain can cause water shortages. Polluted runoff can make water supplies unsafe for drinking and cooking. Higher temperatures have also triggered the growth of **algae** that make water unusable. Salt water from a rising **sea level** is entering *aquifers* (AK wuh fuhrz— areas where water collects underground). Aquifers that supply drinking water to the southern part of the U.S. state of Florida are turning salty.

The largest reservoir in the United States, Lake Mead, has dropped to historic low levels because of a long drought in the western United States. (You can see where the water once would have been by the line on the cliff walls.)

Loss of snow in the Rocky Mountains

During winter, deep snow—a snowpack—piles up atop the Rocky Mountains in the western United States and Canada. When it melts in spring, it provides 85 percent of the water supply for 70 million people. The region the snow waters includes 6 of the 10 fastest growing cities in the United States.

The timing of the snowmelt is key to the water supply. Melting that occurs too early or quickly increases flood danger. It leaves less water for **irrigation** and producing electric power. Without the snowmelt runoff, summer wildfires are more likely.

The timing of the snowmelt is already shifting. Throughout the Rocky Mountains, the spring snowmelt is arriving 10 to 30 days earlier than in the 1950's. Early spring warmth and melting has reduced the snowpack by 20 percent since 1980, according to a government study from 2013. Experts believe that temperatures will increase while snowpack decreases in the years ahead. Meanwhile, as winter temperatures rise, rain increasingly replaces snow. So the snowpack is smaller at the start.

Western communities of Canada and the United States realize that water **conservation** is needed because of the loss of snowpack. Reusing water has become more important.

How do we know?

Scientists have found that the recent decrease in snowpack in the Rocky Mountains is greater than any that occurred in the past 1,000 years. Scientists made a record of past snowpack by examining *tree rings*. For every growing season, a tree adds a layer of wood to its trunk. A *cross-section* (a drawing, diagram, or piece of something cut across) of the trunk shows the layer as a ring. Less wood grows when it is dry, so rings are narrower than those produced in wetter years. Over the most recent decades, narrow tree rings appear, more so than any other time recorded in the studied trunk cross-sections.

Perth combats drought

Perth is a city near the Indian Ocean, tucked away in the southwestern corner of Australia. Perth is Australia's driest and sunniest city. To the east lie low cliffs with a huge desert beyond. Perth has always been very dry. People who live there are used to making the most out of water supplies. In recent years, however, Perth has been drier than dry. Rain—only 0.08 inch (2 millimeters) worth—fell on only three days in the summer of 2014, a record.

Even so, Perth has enough water. Because water has always been scarce, people there are good at managing water supplies. As demand has grown, Perth has developed ways to boost those supplies. Perth is one of the few cities that turns seawater into drinking water. Two *desalination* (dee SAL uh NAY shuhn—salt-removing) plants supply about 40 billion gallons (150 billion liters) of fresh water a year, almost half of Perth's supply. The plants push seawater through a thin material that holds back the salt, producing fresh water.

Water managers in Perth treat waste water until it is safe, then return it to underground storage until needed. By the year 2022, this water deep in the ground will supply about half of Perth's drinking water. Homeowners also store water underground. Buried backyard tanks that collect rain runoff from drainpipes are popular.

A water treatment plant, the Wonthaggi Desalination Plant in the Australian state of Victoria, takes salt water and makes it fresh water.

How we use water

According to most estimates, the average American uses between 80 and 100 gallons (300 and 400 liters) a day. Flushing the toilet takes the most household water. In the typical American home, people use about a gallon (4 liters) a day to brush their teeth. Many dishwashers use 20 gallons (80 liters) daily. But most people in Africa use only 2 to 5 gallons (8 to 20 liters) of water daily.

What can we do?

Climate change may force people to change the way they eat and use water. For many, this will make life more difficult. It may seem like it is impossible to prevent climate change or help sustain Earth's food supply. But, there are many things every one of us can do to help.

Animal farming is one of the biggest sources of gases that are warming Earth like a greenhouse. By eating less meat, people can help reduce these gases. If everyone skipped meat for one day a week, the effect would be huge.

Encourage your family to limit purchases in restaurants and stores to *sustainable* fish. These are types of fish that are caught or farmed in ways that help protect the oceans and the fish they contain.

Conserve water. Ask your family to install a showerhead that reduces water flow. Turn the faucet off while you are brushing your teeth. Use the dishwasher and washing machine only for full loads. These small steps will help save water and even help save money!

GLOSSARY and RESOURCES

algae (singular, alga) Simple living things in oceans, lakes, rivers, ponds, and moist soil. Some algae are tiny and are made up of just one cell, but others are large and contain many cells.

atmosphere The mass of gases that surrounds a planet.

average surface temperature Over a given period—for example, a month—the temperature for each day in the month is totaled and that number is divided by the number of days to get the average.

bacteria A type of simple living thing made of one cell.

carbon dioxide A colorless gas with no smell found in the atmosphere. On Earth, green plants must get carbon dioxide from the atmosphere to live and grow. Animals breathe out the gas when their bodies change food into energy. Carbon dioxide is also created by burning things that contain carbon.

climate The weather of a place averaged over a length of time.

conservation Preserving or protecting from loss.

cyclone A strong storm with winds that spin around the center.

drought When the average rainfall for an area drops far below the normal amount.

ecosystem A complicated system of living things and the environment around them.

fishery A place where many fish are caught.

fossil fuel Coal, oil, or natural gas.

gene The part of a cell that determines which traits living things inherit from their parents. For example, how a leaf is shaped or what eye color a human has are determined by genes.

habitat The kind of place in which a living thing usually makes its home.

irrigation When farmers supply land with water.

LED light Light-emitting diode; a tiny device that gives off light when electric current flows through it.

marsh Low land covered at times by water. Such plants as reeds, rushes, and sedges grow in marshes.

methane A colorless gas with no smell that can be set on fire.

overfishing Catching fish at a rate faster than they can reproduce.

oxygen A chemical element (O) that is one of the most plentiful elements on Earth. Many living things need oxygen to survive. Animals breathe in the gas, where it is used to convert food into energy. Carbon dioxide is then produced as a waste gas.

plateau A raised area of relatively flat land.

predator An animal that eats other animals.

protein One of the three main classes of food; proteins help form muscles.

reservoir A place where water is collected and stored for use.

sea ice Frozen seawater.

sea level The level of the ocean's surface.

storm surge A rapid rise in sea level that happens when winds drive ocean waters ashore.

technology Tools, machines, materials, and ways of doing things that are used to make goods and services and satisfy human needs.

tropics The regions of Earth that lie within about 1,600 miles (2,570 kilometers) north and the same distance south of the equator. The equator is the great circle around Earth that lies halfway between the North and South poles.

Books:

Andregg, Michael. *Seven Billion and Counting: The Crisis in Global Population Growth.* Minneapolis: Twenty-First Century, 2014.

Green, Dan, and Simon Basher. *Climate Change.* New York: Kingfisher, 2014.

Kurlansky, Mark, and Frank Stockton. *World without Fish.* New York: Workman Pub., 2011.

Rothschild, David de. *Earth Matters.* New York: DK Pub., 2011.

Tomecek, Steve. *Global Warming and Climate Change.* New York: Chelsea House, 2012.

Websites:

United States Environmental Protection Agency – A Student's Guide to Global Climate Change
http://www.epa.gov/climatestudents/

United States Environmental Protection Agency – Climate Impacts on Agriculture and Food Supply
http://www.epa.gov/climatechange/impacts-adaptation/agriculture.html

United States Environmental Protection Agency – Climate Impacts on Water Resources
http://www.epa.gov/climatechange/impacts-adaptation/water.html

UN Water – Water and Climate Change
http://www.unwater.org/topics/water-and-climate-change/en/

Think about it:

As water, especially fresh water, becomes more precious, what are some things everyone could do that would, in your opinion, need only a very small *sacrifice* (giving something up)? Would you be willing to sacrifice flushing the toilet every time you used it? Or to turn off the water as you brush your teeth? What kinds of small sacrifices of water might you be willing to make?

INDEX